Zap!

Paint Your Own
GALAXY ROCKS

Alexandra Thomas

hinkler

About this Book

This book contains everything you need to create gorgeous galaxies, cool constellations, and stunning solar systems! It contains eight step-by-step, easy-to-follow projects and all the tools you need to get started on your universe.

Here's everything you'll need to complete these fun projects:

- Rocks
- Paint: black, white, yellow, pink, light purple, dark purple, light blue, blue, dark blue, turquoise, light green, green, tan or light brown
- Sponge or sponge brush
- Stencils
- Pencil and eraser
- Paintbrushes: fine and medium
- Pen

- Clean water in a cup
- Paint palette
- Dotting tools
- Protective finish
- Glow paint (optional)
- Glitter or diamantés (optional)
- Magnets (optional)
- Cardboard (optional)
- Glue (optional)

Published by Hinkler Pty Ltd
45–55 Fairchild Street
Heatherton Victoria 3202 Australia
hinkler www.hinkler.com

© Hinkler Pty Ltd 2023
Images © Hinkler Pty Ltd or Shutterstock.com

Author and artist: Alexandra Thomas
Internal design: Starry Dog Books Ltd
Photography: Alexandra Thomas and Ned Meldrum
Illustration: Brijbasi Art Press Ltd
Prepress: Splitting Image

All rights reserved. No part of this publication may be reproduced, stored in a retrieval system, or transmitted in any way or by any means, electronic, mechanical, photocopying, recording or otherwise, without the prior written permission of Hinkler Pty Ltd.

While every care has been taken in the preparation of this material, the publishers and their respective employees and agents will not accept responsibility for injury or damage occasioned to any person as a result of the activities described in this book.

ISBN: 978 1 4889 5387 3
Printed and bound in China

Contents

Welcome to the Galaxy Rock-painting Universe 4

Sponges 5

Choosing and Working with Paints 7

Marvellous Milky Way 11

Super(nova) Cool Constellations 14

Written in the Stars 16

Cosmic Dragon Egg 18

Up in the Clouds 21

Rock Your World 24

Through the Forest 27

Star Mandala 30

Welcome to the Galaxy Rock-painting Universe

Have you ever gazed up at the night sky and been mesmerised by its inky blackness, which is scattered with luminous stars and swirling bursts of brilliants blues, reds and purples?

Did you ever wish you could create artwork that captured these amazing colours and effects so that you could enjoy them all the time?

With *Paint Your Own Galaxy Rocks*, you'll learn how to create these amazing colour combinations and effects in artworks that can fit into your pocket. You'll be able to turn plain old rocks into your own mini galaxy domes!

Finding the right rocks

The best kind of rocks to paint are smooth, flat and light in colour. These kinds of rocks are mostly found on river beds and some beaches, but they can also be purchased from your local gardening and landscaping stores.

Cleaning your rocks

Some rocks may be dirty or dusty. Even a little layer of dust is problematic, as the paint won't properly adhere to the rock. Cleaning rocks is easy though! Scrub them with a scrubbing brush (or old toothbrush) and warm water with dish soap, then rinse the soap off and place them in a dry, warm area until they are dry. This can take up to 24 hours. Once your rocks are bone-dry, they are ready for painting!

Important

Make sure it is okay to take rocks from an area. Some places have rules to protect the environment against things such as erosion or risks to animal habitats, and in some places, it can also be culturally inappropriate. Make sure you always ask permission before you go rock-hunting on private property.

Sponges

Painting galaxy rocks requires a sponge or a sponge brush to create the best effects.

Choosing sponges

A sponge can be used in many ways to create different effects! Sponge brushes are particularly useful because they give you the texture of a sponge with the dexterity of a brush. Their different sides allow for smaller and larger areas of paint application and allow you to create different effects. Sponge brushes come in a range of shapes and sizes and are commonly available in arts and crafts stores.

Dish sponges and make-up sponges (which come in handy triangle shapes) are cheap and available in a variety of sizes, shapes, textures and levels of absorption (how much liquid – in this case paint – they can soak up). These qualities affect how the sponges apply paint to the rock and the end result. Because sponges are soft, they can be easily trimmed to create another shape or size, which is helpful when trying to paint small spaces or create a different effect. Make sure to ask an adult before using scissors for anything!

It is super handy to have more than one sponge and more than one type of sponge on hand when you are creating galaxy rock art so you can experiment with different styles!

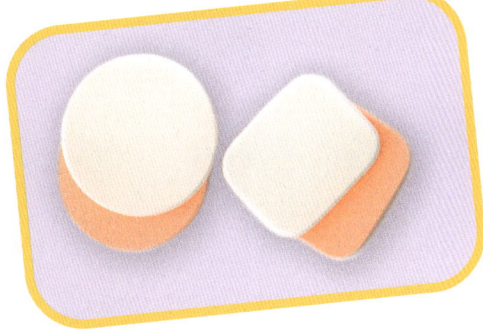

Sponging techniques

How you use your sponge varies depending on the effect you're trying to achieve. Sometimes you will require a paint palette, which can be an actual palette from an arts and crafts store or just a spare plate (porcelain is best) or piece of cardboard.

Have a piece of scrap paper nearby to dab with your sponge and paint – this way you can check the size, shape and colour you'll get before applying it to your rock. A spare rock in the same colour as the one you are using for the project is also useful – if you're painting the rock black, do this to your spare rock too, to test your colours.

Use the palette before painting on the rock to reduce the amount of paint on the sponge. This is great for getting rid of excess paint and for blending (see page 8 for more on this technique).

The amount of pressure that you apply to the sponge also creates different effects. Lightly dabbing with the sponge will produce lighter marks than pushing hard. You can see in the rock below that the lighter blue ring has pressed more lightly and with more of the sponge surface than the more concentrated, thinner purple ring.

Handy Hint
Remember to clean your sponge and paintbrushes after each project and between steps if needed. This will keep you from unintentionally blending colours on the rock and stop paint from drying hard on the sponge, making it difficult to remove later.

Choosing and Working with Paints

For painting galaxy artwork on rocks, you will need to use acrylic paint. Commonly available craft paint (or 'student-grade' acrylic paint) works really well. It dries fast and sticks well to a rock's surface.

Most galaxy art uses a variety of purples, blues, pinks and greens, and these are great colours to start with. But you can also add reds, yellows and oranges, and some are a combination of all colours – it's all up to what you want your galaxy to look like!

Handy Hint
Make sure that you always thoroughly cover your clothes and working space before creating your galaxy rock art, as it can get messy.

Mixing paint colours

If you don't have all the colours you need, you can mix some colours to make others. For example, if you need a colour to be lighter, try adding a small dash of white. You can add white to red to create pink colours. Don't add too much white at once though, or you will wash the colour out. You can always add more as you need.

Adding a touch of black will also darken colours – just be careful to add only a very tiny bit at a time, or it will quickly become muddy in colour.

Get some extra paint in the primary colours – that is, red, blue and yellow – as these can be mixed to create a range of other colours:

red + yellow = orange

blue + yellow = green

blue + red = purple

Blending paint colours

1. To blend multiple colours, use a sponge and a paintbrush. Use a paintbrush to apply a colour to one side of the sponge.
Then clean your brush and apply the colour you want to blend directly next to the first colour on the sponge.

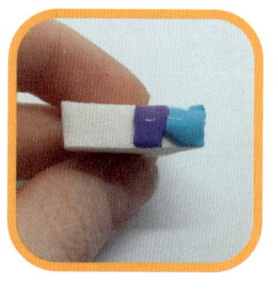

2. Dab the sponge on your palette to get rid of excess paint.

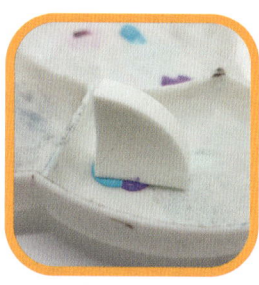

3. Select a clean area of the palette and dab your sponge again.

4. Dab multiple times in the same spot until you see the colours start to blend.

5. Once the two colours are blended on the palette, you'll be able to see the colours blending on the sponge as well.

6. Dabbing up or down will give you different blends.

7. If you run out of paint or it starts drying on the sponge, use the excess paint you dabbed off the sponge at the start to continue with the blend.

This process can be done with as many colours as will fit on the sponge.

Handy Hint
Make sure that you allow each layer of paint to dry completely before you handle your rock or paint any other layers on top, otherwise you might cause smudges.

Other types of paint and craft materials

Once you have all your basic supplies, you may also want some extra paint and crafting materials to lift your galaxy rocks to the next level. Try glow-in-the-dark acrylic paint, glitter and stick-on gems to make your rocks sparkle!

Creating stars

Stars are an essential part of galaxy rock art. There are a few different ways you can create them.

Paintbrush hand-dotting

Paint in your dots one by one with a thin paintbrush. This way you can be precise about how many stars you want, where you want them, and what you want them to look like. But this can take a long time and leave you with speckles that are not very round.

Flicking

1. To flick, you need to thin your paint. Add a little water to your palette alongside your white paint.
2. Mix a drop of white paint with a drop of water on your palette until you have a thin, white liquid.
3. Use a fine paintbrush to pick the liquid up.
4. Practise flicking the paint onto a piece of paper until you are happy with the size of your star dots. Then hold your paintbrush horizontally over the rock and tap the side of it firmly several times. Little droplets will fly off and create a great star effect! The smaller the brush used for flicking, the smaller the stars.

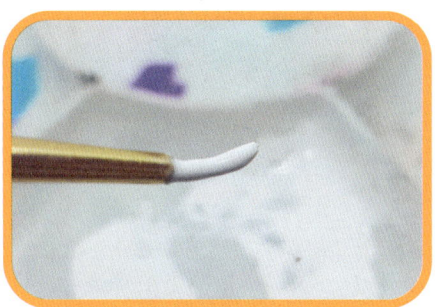

Handy Hint
Make sure to prepare your area with a towel or sheet first or do this somewhere outside as it can be very messy! Younger rock painters should ask an adult for assistance.

Paintbrush crosses

1. To make a star pop, select a larger dot to paint over with your brush.

2. Thin your paint down with a drop of water and wipe the excess off on a piece of tissue or paper towel to help you create super-thin lines.

3. Using the very tip of your paintbrush, make a long cross shape by painting a long, vertical line and a shorter horizontal line in white over the middle of the dot.

4. Then paint a very small x over the top of the cross.

Dotting tools

Make round dots using items around the house, such as toothpicks, pencil tips, bobby pins or anything else with a rounded tip! Dotting tools can be bought from arts and craft stores or online. Always get an adult's permission before purchasing anything online.

Sealing

To preserve your galaxy art, use a protective finish. Sealing agents can be bought from hardware and craft stores in paint-on and spray-on forms and come in gloss or matte. Use a waterproof sealant if the rocks will be outside. Let your rock dry completely before using the protective finish. Leave the finish to dry for at least 24 hours.

Handy Hint
Protective finishes can contain harmful chemicals. Always ask an adult to help you when using a sealing agent. When using a spray-on finish, always work outside or in a well-ventilated room, and make sure to spray away from yourself.

Marvellous Milky Way

Simply stunning, this Milky Way will make you feel like you're in the sky among the stars...

1. Use a medium-sized brush to paint the front and sides of your rock black.

2. Use the sponge to dab dark purple on the left-hand side of the rock in patches. Only apply paint to the sponge once: as it starts to dry and the patches get smaller, blend them into the black background, keeping to the left-hand side.

3. Use the same sponge to apply dark blue paint through the centre of the rock in the same way as in step 2. As the blue paint on your sponge starts to dry, add some smaller patches on the left, overlapping some of the purple to help blend the patches.

You Will Need
- Rock
- Medium paintbrush
- Paint – black, dark purple, dark blue, dark green, light purple, light blue, light green, white
- Sponge brush
- Thin paintbrush

4. Repeat step 3 on the right-hand side of the rock with the dark green. As the paint dries, place some green patches through the blue to help blend them. The more paint on your sponge, the brighter the colours will look, so be careful not to use too much.

11

5. Once the base colours are done, start the highlights. Use a clean sponge to pick up some light purple paint and dab it on your palette a few times until the patches are small. Then dab over the top of the purple patches on the rock, making sure you leave some of the darker purple showing underneath.

8. Add some stars by using the flick technique with white paint (see page 9 for instructions on the flicking method).

6. Using the same sponge, repeat this process with light blue paint over the darker blue patches, making sure you leave some of the dark blue showing.

7. With the same sponge, repeat this process with light green paint over the darker green patches, making sure you leave some of the dark green showing underneath.

9. Find a very light patch of colour on the rock to add big, sparkly stars. Paint a small dot, then add a cross and an x with your brush (see page 10 for instructions on creating paintbrush crosses).

Handy Hint
Use lighter coloured sponges so you can easily see the quantity and colour of paint you've applied.

10. Add a moon by painting a white circle. You may have to go over the white a couple of times to make sure no colour shows through. Make sure you wait for the paint to dry between layers.

11. Complete your moon by using the tip of a sponge to pick up a small amount of black paint. Dab your sponge on the palette until there are only a few specks of black showing, then dab directly on to the moon a few times to create the illusion of craters and shadows!

Did You Know?
The Milky Way is shaped like a spiral and rotates in space like a pinwheel. It takes around 230 million years for our Solar System to travel just once around the centre of the Milky Way!

Super(nova) Cool Constellations

Make your very own out-of-this-world constellation or re-create your star sign and keep it with you for astrological good luck!

1. Sponge black paint onto your rock for the background, adding more at the bottom of the rock than the top. Don't worry about placement or accidently sponging too much black: your colours will still show up over black, just not as brightly as over the blank part of the rock.

You Will Need
- Light-coloured rock
- Sponge brush
- Paint – black, pink, purple, dark blue, teal, light blue, white
- Fine paintbrush

4. Dip your clean sponge into the dark blue and the teal to create a mixed blue effect and apply to the top blank parts of the rock. Bring one side of the blue paint mix down to meet a patch of purple.

2. Once the black paint has dried, use a clean sponge to add pink on the blank patches at the bottom of the rock. Overlap some onto the black. The black under the pink makes a purple colour, which helps with blending in the next step.

3. Blend purple with the pink. Use the same sponge you used for the pink (see page 8 for more on blending). Keep the purple colour around the middle and bottom of the rock.

5. Use the same sponge to place a lighter blue over some of the mixed blue for a glowing effect. Now you have all your background colours.

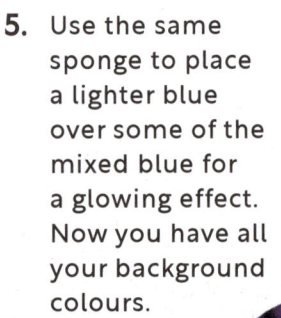

14

6. To create a darker background for your constellation to show up brightly, sponge some black through the middle and in any remaining blank spots on the rock. You can also use it to cover any unwanted colours.

7. Add some stars. These will be joined up in step 8. You can use the flick technique to create stars (see page 9) or you can paint stars at random or in positions that re-create your own star sign!

8. Once you have chosen which stars to use for your constellations, add straight lines between them, like in a dot-to-dot puzzle. You now have your own unique sky of star formations!

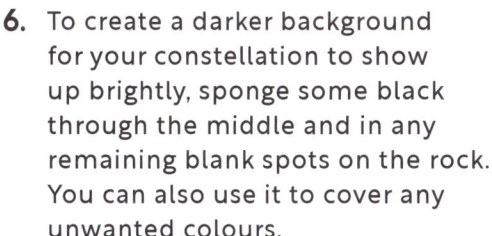

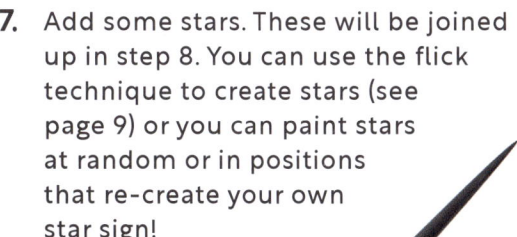

Handy Hint
Add some glow paint over the top of your stars and constellation lines for a cool effect that really shines.

Written in the Stars

Smaller rocks are great for this project as you can make multiple letters and link them together to create words or phrases!

1. Using your pencil, sketch a letter in the centre of your rock. Go over the pencil in pen. Once the pen ink has dried, erase the pencil from underneath.

2. Use black paint and a fine paintbrush to colour the insides of the letter. If you are drawing freehand, don't worry too much about going over the lines, as that can be fixed in later steps.

You Will Need
- Rock
- Pencil
- Permanent black fine-liner pen
- Eraser
- Paint — black, blue, green, white
- Fine paintbrush
- Sponge brush or small sponge
- Medium paintbrush
- Stencil (optional)

4. Mix your white paint with the green paint and then mix white with blue, making a light green paint and a light blue paint. Use these colours to lightly sponge over the top of their matching darker paint to create a slight glow effect.

5. Once you are happy with your colours, use the flick technique to create stars (see page 9). Remember: the smaller the brush used for flicking, the smaller the stars.

3. When the black paint is dry, use a sponge brush or small sponge to paint blue and green patches on your letter.

16

6. Use your fine paintbrush to bring a single shining star to life! Paint a bigger dot with your brush, then add a cross and an x (see page 10).

8. To finish it off, add a thin white line around the outline of the letter. This will make it really pop out from the black background and will clearly show your beautiful colours and stars!

7. If you are using a stencil, remove it now. Use your medium-sized paintbrush to paint the blank area of the rock black, covering any wonky lines or colour spillage. Your letter may start to blend in with the background, but there should still be an obvious outline, due to the stars and colours.

Try This!

Try making a plaque to hang on your bedroom door by using the letters of your name, a piece of cardboard, a piece of string and superglue. Glue one end of the string on the top left side of the cardboard and the other end on the top right side. When dry, glue your letter rocks to the cardboard and wait for them to dry. You now have a name plaque!

Cosmic Dragon Egg

Something's about to hatch! Bring a rounded rock to life with this cracking cosmic dragon egg!

1. Prepare your rock surface by sponging white paint over the front.

2. With a clean sponge, paint the entire back of the rock black. As you come around the front of the rock with the black, leave an oval shape in the centre. This space will be where most of your colour goes.

You Will Need
- Egg-shaped rock
- Paint – white, black, dark blue, light blue, purple, pink, yellow
- Sponge
- Fine paintbrush

3. Using a clean sponge, repeatedly dab around the line between the black and white paint with dark blue. As the paint on your sponge starts to dry, sponge some blue patches on the black surrounding the outside of the rock, for a diluted dark blue effect.

Handy Hint
To make super-thin lines, try dipping your paintbrush in water and then straight into a small drop of paint. Mix it thoroughly until the texture is creamy – not liquid. This will make the brush tip more pointed and the paint glide more smoothly.

4. If your sponge has a lot of blue paint left on it, clean it with water or use a new one. If your sponge is dry, use the same one to pick up some light blue paint. Sponge a smaller light blue oval shape within the dark blue, overlapping the colours until you have a thin edge of dark blue. Make sure to leave enough white space for the next few colours.

Handy Hint
To make super-thin lines, try to keep your sponges dry to ensure the colours are as vibrant as possible. Water on the sponge can lift or blend with the paint underneath.

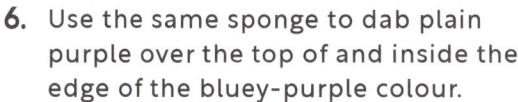

7. Repeat step 5 with purple paint and pink paint. Keep the mixed section mostly pink, so it blends with the yellow in step 8. Sponge the pink/purple mix around the inside of the purple on the stone, keeping a small white space for the last burst of colour.

5. Use your paintbrush to pick up some purple and mix it with the light blue until you have a bluey-purple colour. Clean your brush afterwards. Use a sponge to dab your new colour around the inside and over the top of the light blue shape.

8. Once your sponge is dry, pick up some yellow paint and dab it into the last white patch.

6. Use the same sponge to dab plain purple over the top of and inside the edge of the bluey-purple colour.

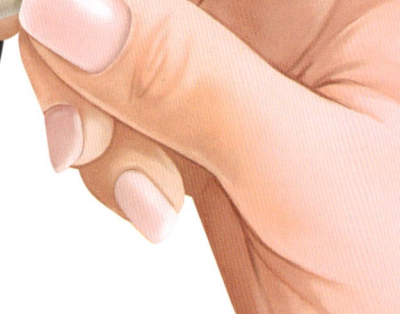

19

9. Now you have your cosmic background colours, add the stars using the flick technique (see page 9). Your cosmic dragon egg is now complete!

10. But wait – it's hatching! For a cool effect, add some black lines with a thin paintbrush to create cracks, as if your egg is about to explode with a baby cosmic dragon!

Handy Hint
Try some other spectacular colours for your dragon eggs. Some great combinations are:
- green, blue, purple and pink
- yellow, orange and red
- blue, green, yellow, orange and red
- pink, purple and blue

Up in the Clouds

Gaze up at the moon and the starry sky through a break in the clouds with this dreamy scene!

1. Using a sponge, paint black where you want the night sky. It's better to do a little extra black than not enough, as you will be going over the edges with white later. If you don't have a white rock, let the black dry and add white paint on the remaining part of the rock.

2. With a clean sponge, dab dark blue paint in random spots in the night sky. Dab the paint on a piece of cardboard or a paint palette a few times first to get rid of excess paint before sponging the rock. Without cleaning the sponge, dip light blue into the middle of the dark blue patches to create a glowing effect.

You Will Need
- White or light-coloured rock
- Sponge
- Paint — black, white (if don't have a light-coloured rock), dark blue, light blue, white, purple, pink
- Piece of scrap card/paper or a paint palette
- Paintbrush

3. Use the flick technique to create some stars in your night sky (see page 9).

4. Randomly sponge some dark blue inside your clouds, keeping away from the night sky edge. You can use the same sponge from step 2. Remember to dab your sponge a few times to remove excess paint before applying it to rock. These dark patches form some of the underside of your clouds.

5. Using the same sponge and keeping any remaining blue paint on it, randomly dab some purple on to your clouds. This will help blend the colours.

6. Repeat step 5 with the same sponge, this time adding pink. Try to leave some white near the top of the white space for the tops of your clouds.

7. It's fluff time! Using a clean sponge, apply white to the blank spaces. As the paint on your sponge dries, add some white patches to your coloured sections too. This will dull the brightness of the colours, making them softer and more pastel.

8. Start forming your cloud shapes with white paint. Use your paintbrush to create the shapes, following the mostly white patches. Make sure the white goes just over the night sky, so there are no gaps between the sky and the clouds.

9. Once all the cloud shapes are clear, sponge white inside the edges of the tops of each cloud. You can also do this with a brush if you feel it gives you more control.

Did You Know?

A cloud is a large collection of densely packed particles of water or ice that is suspended in the atmosphere of a planet. Clouds around Earth are formed when water evaporates into the sky and then condenses into water vapour when it hits cooler air higher up in the atmosphere.

10. Finish your cloudy night sky with a moon! Make a circle with your brush and white paint, then fill it in with white.

> ### Try This!
> As a cool extension project, try gluing a magnet to the back of your stone to make a galactic fridge attachment!

Now you are ready to rock on cloud nine!

Rock Your World

Have the whole world in your hands as you learn how to rock everyone's world with this perfect planetary design!

1. With a pencil, sketch a large circle in the centre of your rock. Trace over the pencil in fine-liner pen. Wait for the pen to dry and then erase the pencil underneath.

2. Using a medium-sized paintbrush, paint the outside of the circle in black.

You Will Need

- Rock
- Pencil
- Permanent black fine-liner pen
- Eraser
- Medium paintbrush
- Paint – black, purple, white, green, tan or light brown, dark blue
- Sponge
- Fine paintbrush
- Piece of cardboard/paint palette

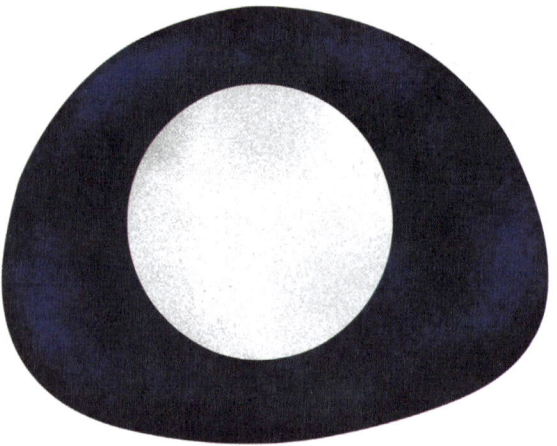

3. Use your sponge to place purple around the outside of the rock, making sure to stay on the black parts only. The purple splotches don't need to be in any particular placement or order; just try not to cover too much of the black.

Handy Hint
Use a stencil or something round to trace a perfect circle. You can use a world stencil for doing the land shapes as well.

4. Add stars to your background using the flick technique with white paint (see page 9).

5. Use green paint to create landmasses within your world! You can base the shapes on a globe or create your own world by placing green wherever you like. Ensure you leave enough space for the following steps.

6. Use tan paint to create dirt within and around the landmasses. Go over the edges of the green paint with the tan to create a blended colour. Don't worry if the green paint is wet or dry at this stage, as tan is usually translucent and will blend even when dry.

7. Now add the ocean. Use dark blue to paint the remaining blank parts of your rock, making sure to get into all the gaps between the land.

8. To create wispy clouds, pick up a very small amount of white paint with the tip of your sponge. You can cut your sponge to shape if you need to. Sponge your palette a few times until only a little paint is left on the sponge, then apply it to your world wherever you wish. Keep all the white within the planet but don't worry about going over the land parts (once they have dried), as that's what clouds do!

Handy Hint

For extra ideas and inspiration, try searching online for images of the Earth, or you could even create your own version by making unique continents and islands straight from your imagination!

25

9. Add solid fluffy clouds using a thin paintbrush to apply white paint in patches. Again, stay within the planet and don't worry about going over the land. If you do go over the edges a little, clean it up with black paint once the white is dry.

Try This!
You don't have to be bound by Earth. You can pick your favourite planet, or create an amazing sky of planets! Saturn with its rings is always a classic.

10. To make your planet stand out from the dark background, add a thin white line around it using your thin brush. You can now hold the whole world in your hand!

Welcome to the blue planet. Your mission is complete!

Through the Forest

Wander through a green wonderland and gaze up at the night sky through the dark trees with this atmospheric rock.

1. Create a mystical night sky by sponging black on each side of the rock, leaving a long triangular shape down the middle of the stone unpainted.

2. With a new sponge, paint a white layer over the blank area of your rock and over the edges of the black paint so it blends. Maintain the triangular shape.

You Will Need
- Rock
- Sponge
- Fine paintbrush
- Paint – black, white, green, light green, yellow

4. With the same sponge, dab a light green down the middle of the dark green triangular patch, leaving some of the darker green exposed. The background will start to glow a little!

5. With a paintbrush, mix a very small portion of light green paint with yellow paint, so the yellow has a greenish tinge. Sponge it down the centre of the triangular patch. Make it a thin enough line so that all three colours are visible, as this will help create the glow effect.

3. Use a clean sponge to dab green paint over the white patch, covering it completely. Sponge green paint around the black sporadically, leaving some black patches. The green will look darker on the black background than on the white.

6. Now it's time for the stars! Try one of the techniques on pages 9–10 to create your stars.

8. Starting from the top of the middle tree trunk, use a thin paintbrush to create leaves. Make small downward and outward strokes from the centre of each trunk. It's fine if the trees overlap, as that's what they do in real life too!

7. Now the glowing night sky is finished, it's time to add a forest. Paint a series of thin black lines along the bottom and up the sides of the rock, some short and some long. These will be the tree trunks. Along the sides, angle the trees inwards so that all the tree tops face towards the centre. This will create the illusion of looking up through the trees into the night sky.

9. Add a single sparkling star to set the scene! Paint a bigger dot with your brush, then add a cross and an x (see page 10).

28

Try This!
Instead of trees, try creating some building silhouettes underneath a city sky! You can even add glow paint to the windows to make them light up in the dark.

Well done! Your trip through the starlit forest is complete!

Star Mandala

Your final journey into creating out-of-this-world art is creating this challenging but spectacular star mandala!

1. With your pencil, draw a star shape. Go over the top of it with pen and erase the pencil underneath.

2. Fill in your star with black paint using a fine brush. Try not to go over the edges!

3. Place the tip of your largest dotting tool in your dark blue paint and make a dot in the middle of the star. Clean your dotting tool and place 5 light blue dots around the centre dot.

You Will Need
- Rock
- Sponge
- Fine paintbrush
- Paint — black, dark blue, light blue, light purple, pink, dark purple, white, grey (optional)
- Dotting tools — small, medium and large (see pictures for proportional dot width). You can get these tools either from an art store or see page 10 for other options)

4. Using the medium dotting tool, place 6 light-purple dots around each of the light-blue dots. Every time you start a new set of 6 dots, re-dip your dotting tool in the purple paint. As you dot repeatedly with one tool, the dots get smaller!

> **Did You Know?**
> The Sun is the closest star to Earth and is 109 times wider than Earth.

9. Add some extra dots on top of other dots, wherever you like!.

10. For extra pizzazz, add a shadow to your star mandala! You can do this by mixing your white and black paint until you have a dark grey then applying it to the left-hand side of your star sides, like the picture.

5. Use the same travelling dot technique with pink paint. Start your dots above and between your first and second purple dots.

6. Repeat again with dark blue and a bigger dotting tool. Note: you may only be able to fit in 4 or 5 dots now as your space gets smaller.

7. Using the smallest dotting tool, repeat the same technique with light blue, then purple. Then start again with dark blue, and continue the colour cycle until you almost reach the points of the star. Place one white dot at the end of each star point.

8. Using white on your small dotting tool, place some dots in the middle of your largest dark blue dots. Add 2 small white dots under your original white dots at the end of each star point.